This book is in memory of:

_____

My most cherished memories are:

_____
_____
_____
_____
_____
_____
_____
_____
_____
_____

Dedications

To my husband who was the creator and inspiration behind this story and our beautiful girls who remind me of Nana Rosie everyday. I hope to develop the same amazing relationship with you girls that I had with my Mom. Keep watching for those rainbows of hope!
—Colleen C. Ster

To my loving husband, "magical" Noelle, and "precious" Anna: I believe in you.
—Lynn Dubenko, Ph.D.

I dedicate this book to my Mom, my biggest cheerleader. I am thankful for her example of simple living, fun personality, and warmth.
—Amy McClenahan

I dedicate this book to Christopher, my brother and buddy, whose short life has deepened my heart of compassion.
—Mike McClenahan

Charity

A portion of sales from this book will be donated to the KidsGames program at Solana Beach Presbyterian Church for children to attend this values-based sports camp.

Inspiration

"Always be joyful. Keep on praying. No matter what happens, always be thankful for this is God's will for you..."
— 1 Thessalonians 5:16-18

The Holy Bible, New Living Translation, BibleStudyTools.com, 1996

And God said, "This is the covenant I am making between me and you and every living creature with you, a covenant for all generations to come: I have set my rainbow in the clouds, and it will be the sign of the covenant between me and the earth. Whenever I bring clouds over the earth and the rainbow appears in the clouds, I will remember my covenant between me and you and all living creatures of every kind..."
—Genesis 9:12-15

"To him who overcomes, I will give the right to sit with me on my throne... After this I looked, and there before me was a door standing open in heaven... At once I was in the Spirit, and there before me was a throne in heaven with someone sitting on it...A rainbow...encircled the throne."
—Revelation 3:21, 4:1-3

The Quest Study Bible, New International Version, Grand Rapids: Zondervan Publishing House, 1984

REMIND ME AGAIN

by The Ster Family
Illustrated by Colleen C. Ster
along with Lynn
Dubenko, Ph.D., and
Mike and Amy
McClenahan

Published by Reflections Publishing
© 2011 Reflections Publishing.

First Edition. Published in the United States of America.

ISBN 978-1-61660-001-3

Visit our web site at www.reflectionspublishing.com for more information or inquiries.

* * *

Other books by Reflections Publishing:

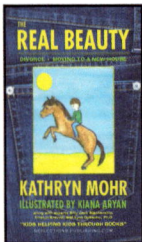

The Real Beauty - ISBN: 978-1-61660-000-6
Written by: Kathryn Mohr
Illustrated by: Kiana Aryan

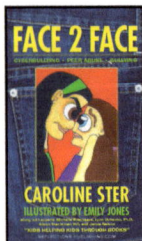

Face 2 Face - ISBN: 978-1-61660-002-0
Written by: Caroline Ster
Illustrated by: Emily Jones

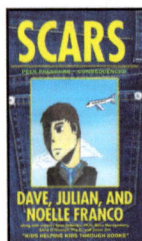

Scars - ISBN: 978-1-61660-003-7
Written and Illustrated by Parent/Child Team:
Dave, Julian, and Noelle Franco

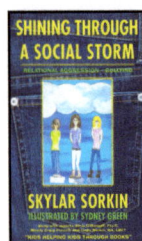

Shining Through a Social Storm - ISBN: 978-1-61660-004-4
Written by: Skylar Sorkin
Illustrated by: Sydney Green

Foreword
By Diane Pearson, Author of
God in the Midst of Grief: 101 True Stories of Comfort

When Colleen Ster asked me to write the foreword for this book, I thought it would be difficult. You see, the subject of the book, "Nana" (Rosie), was my best friend for thirty-five years. She died at age fifty-nine, much too young for those of us who loved her so much. But as I read the manuscript, instead of tears, it brought smiles, especially the last drawing in the book with the circular rainbow.

One of the stories in my book, *God in the Midst of Grief*, is about Rosie and a circular rainbow. Rosie told me several stories throughout our long friendship of rainbows appearing at special times in her life, usually as a source of comfort. It was no surprise, then that a rainbow appeared after her funeral.

Rosie's family and friends said their final good-byes at the cemetery and headed back to their small country church for the funeral dinner. As they headed west, one of the grandkids looked out the car window excitedly and said, "Look at that rainbow! Have you ever seen a rainbow like that?"

Witnesses said it was not a "normal" rainbow with an arc across the sky; instead, it encircled the sun, like a halo, and then there was a second circular rainbow out farther from the first. It was fainter, almost like a shadow of the first rainbow.

As they watched the spectacle on their drive back to the church, Rosie's husband, Jerry, said, "I asked for a sign that she was in heaven. That's it." What a wonderful story to pass on to Rosie's grandchildren!

As you read this book to your children, grandchildren, or other special children in your life, let it be a beginning point of conversation about the death of someone close to them. Ask the child to recall a favorite time with that person, and then fill in the blanks with true stories they can relate to and will bring fond memories.

Remind Me Again demonstrates a powerful, yet simple, way for children to keep the memory of a beloved grandparent or family member alive—bedtime stories celebrating the unique qualities of the grandparent and how those qualities live on in the life of the child.

As a leader of grief support groups and classes on various topics related to grief, I plan to recommend *Remind Me Again* as a straightforward, emotionally healthy way for children to remember their grandparents or other loved ones.

Grief is the price we pay for love. It is inescapable. Children, as well as adults, need constructive ways to cope with grief. *Remind Me Again* will help grieving children redirect their thoughts to memories they can cherish.

"Bedtime," Daddy announced as I bounced into my room.

"Five more minutes?" I pleaded as Daddy cleared off my stuffed animals.

"How about we read a story, honey?" Daddy replied.

I scrunched my face— hoping for something a little different tonight. "Instead of reading a story, Daddy, could you tell me a story?"

"Oooo, good idea," Daddy said. "Do you want to be a lovely princess who dances with a handsome prince? Or perhaps a magical fairy who saves the kingdom from an evil sorcerer?"

"Not tonight, Dad. Tonight, before you tuck me in, could you..."

"Could I what?" Daddy asked as he pulled back my rose-covered blankets.

I swallowed hard, and asked, "Could you, will you please, remind me again about Nana?"

Daddy stopped what he was doing and stared into my eyes. I think he was trying to decide if I really wanted to hear about Nana, or if I just wanted to stay up a little later.

I would never admit it to Daddy, but maybe it was a little of both. While I couldn't be sure, I thought I detected a hint of a smile on Daddy's face.

"Okay," Daddy said.

"Hooray," I shouted.

"What would you like to know this time?" Daddy asked.

"Well, this time remind me why we liked Nana," I said. "Loved, I meant loved," I said as my face turned fire-engine red.

"I knew what you meant," Daddy said. "Now, where should I start? There were so many reasons why we loved Nana. We loved Nana because she was always full of enthusiasm."

"What's en-tu-see-as-um?" I said, trying my best to pronounce such a big word.

"Enthusiasm," Daddy repeated. "It means Nana was excited about everything. Nana was a ball of energy."

"A ball of energy, huh?" I said jumping up and down on my bed. "You know, Mom says I have enough energy to light a small city."

"You don't say," Daddy replied. "I hadn't noticed, but, honey, could you please stop doing cartwheels on your bed?"

I finished my pajama gymnastics (receiving high scores from all the stuffed-animal judges in my room) and sat down next to Daddy.

"As I was saying," he continued, "Nana was always excited about life and had lots of energy."

"That sounds like me," I said.

"Yes, just like you," Daddy replied.

"What else did we love about Nana?"

"Well," Daddy began, "Nana liked to try new things. She loved adventure, traveling to far off places, playing new games, and even trying new foods."

"Hey, that sounds like me too," I said. "Except..."

"Except what?" Daddy asked.

"Except, I don't like to eat vegetables, especially lima beans."

"You know, I'm pretty sure Nana didn't like lima beans either," Daddy said. "In fact, Nana once told me she hid her vegetables, especially her lima beans, under her plate when she was exactly your age. Does that sound familiar?"

"Wow, that does sounds like me," I said.

"Yep, just like you."

"Nana also loved to lead cheers," Daddy said.

"Cheers for what?" I asked.

"She loved to cheer during ball games or games we played at home, but she especially—"

"Especially what?" I asked excitedly.

"Well, Nana especially loved to lead cheers for you, princess. Nana cheered for everything you did."

My very own cheerleader, I thought. Interesting, but I wanted more details from Daddy.

"Like what?" I asked.

"Like, when you learned to walk for the first time," Daddy said. "Nana never cheered so happily. In fact, after you took your first steps, she clapped and cheered so loud, you fell down laughing."

I pondered this for a few moments. "You know, I love to cheer too. Remember that cheerleading camp last summer? I loved it! Of all the kids, I cheered the loudest."

"I know. You reminded me of Nana as you yelled each word."

"Huh," I said, "that does sound like me."

"Yes, just like you."

"Nana also loved to sing," Daddy said. "She always had a song in her heart. No matter where Nana was, or what she was doing, Nana sang right out loud. And when other people heard her, it made them want to sing along."

"Gee, Dad, I love to sing all the time too."

"Nana also loved to put on shows for our family. She would play dress-up with you kids in fancy clothes with sparkles, or funny clothes with crazy colors that didn't match, and you all would sing and dance until you were all laughing together."

"Daddy, you know how much I love to play dress-up and pretend I am a princess who sings beautiful songs," I said. "That really sounds like me."

"Yes, just like you."

Daddy looked down at his watch, which I knew meant our story was about to end. "We only have time for one more reason why we loved Nana, but it's my favorite," Daddy said.

"What is it?"

"Nana always made us feel loved."

"How'd she do that?"

"I'm not exactly sure how she did that," Daddy said with a puzzled look on his face. "Nana could somehow create magic out of thin air with just a look, a smile, a few kind words, or a hug. Nana made everyone feel right at home. Nana made everyone feel safe. Somehow, your Nana always made everyone feel loved."

"That sure sounds nice," I said clutching my favorite teddy bear.

"It really was," Daddy said. "And, you know what, kiddo? It's the way I feel when I'm with you."

"With me, Dad? Really?"

"Yes, with you. Really."

When I heard that, I dropped my bear and hugged Daddy as tight as I could. "Well then, that sounds like me too, Daddy."

"Yes, just like you."

As Daddy tucked me in bed and gave me a kiss on the cheek, I tried to close my eyes (so I could dream a very pleasant dream about my Nana), but my eyes weren't quite ready to cooperate.

So instead of going to sleep, I looked up at Daddy and said, "Nana really sounds wonderful."

"She was, honey."

"Daddy, if Nana was so wonderful, why is it so hard for me to remember her?" Daddy studied my face, which meant I had asked a tough question. I wasn't worried, though, because my Daddy knows everything.

"Because, my sweet princess," Daddy finally said. "You were, and are, so young. Your mind is filled each and every day with the lovely thoughts of childhood: the thrill of bike riding, the joy of chocolate ice cream with sprinkles, and the happiness of jumping rope with friends."

"But, Dad," I said. "I don't ever want to forget Nana. I want to remember everything about her. Just the possibility that I might totally forget Nana makes me sad." Trying my best not to cry, I said, "Daddy, do you promise to always help me remember Nana?"

"I promise, sweetheart," Daddy said. "I will continue to tell you stories about Nana every time you ask, even when it's past bedtime. I will never let you forget your Nana."

This made me feel a little better, but something still bothered me.

"Why are you scrunching your cute little face again, honey?" Daddy asked.

"Well, Dad, what if you forget about Nana?"

"I will never forget about Nana."

"But, how can you be so sure?"

"Because, sleepy head, whenever I want to remember Nana, all I have to do is look at you. You remind me of Nana every day with your warm smile, your amazing sense of adventure, your beautiful songs, your boundless energy, your magical joy, and especially your great big hugs."

Before I finally drifted off to sleep, I gave Daddy another great big hug and said, "Yeah, Dad, that sounds like me too."

"Yes, honey it does sound like you," Daddy whispered. "Just like you."

4114U

(Information For You!)

Written by:
Lynn Dubenko, Ph.D. - Child/Family Psychologist
Amy McClenahan - Educator
Mike McClenahan - Senior Pastor
Colleen C. Ster - Research/Development/Illustrations

Kids: When you experience the passing of a grandparent or family member, it can be very upsetting. You may feel like an earthquake has hit your family. The foundation that you have known since the day you were born is being shaken, stirred, and torn apart. When an earthquake occurs out in the ocean it creates a tsunami of high waves. The emotions that you may feel during the grieving process are very similar to waves crashing along the shoreline. When the death first happens, you may feel like you just got hit by a tsunami wave. You might feel better for a couple of days and then out of nowhere another big wave may come to shore and knock you down. As you work your way through the grieving process you will experience many different types of waves.

Just know that how you are feeling is very normal and over time you will overcome your grief and find acceptance in your loss. Keep talking to your parents because these feelings can be very overwhelming for an adult, but even harder for a child to process. So just remember to keep communicating with family, friends, and especially with your parents as you go through these normal stages of grief.

The stages that you may find yourself going though will include:

1. **Denial: This can't be happening.**
2. **Anger: This is NOT fair!**
3. **Bargaining: It can work out.**
4. **Depression: Leave me alone.**
5. **Acceptance: Life is good again.**

Parents: Grief and loss are normal and essential parts of the human experience. They come from the ability to love and care for others. Like strong ocean waves, loss will knock you down and you may feel like you are drowning in a sea of memories and emotions. If you fight this experience and swim against those waves, they will only carry you further from the shore and wear you down. By reading through the following 4114U section with your child, hopefully you can all navigate through all those waves of grief, big and small, and land safely back on shore.

Keepsake Idea

You can glue an envelope in the back of this book to store treasured keepsakes, notes, special photographs, and holiday family recipes. Special recipes such as the sweet potato casserole always made for Thanksgiving, or the chocolate sheet cake for birthdays, or the sugar cookie recipe for the holidays can bring back treasured memories that over time will be warm and comforting.

Action Steps to Help Families Emotionally

Written by Lynn Dubenko, Ph.D. - Child/Family Psychologist

Many are familiar with the Five Stages of Grief, as defined by Elizabeth Kubler-Ross.
1. Denial ⇨ **2. Anger** ⇨ **3. Bargaining** ⇨ **4. Depression** ⇨ **5. Acceptance**

In some circumstances, particularly among children though, the stages of grief may look a little different. You might see that your child experiences the following stages:

• **Disbelief:** difficulty believing that your loved one is gone and imagining daily life or special events without them.

• **Emotional Reaction:** this may include anger, sadness, fear, and anxiety, among other emotions. You might notice changes in overall mood, behavior, socialization, school performance, and physical health.
   ⇨ Dealing with their own emotions: Allow your child to express anger and sadness regarding the loss, as well as, their fears and anxiety about losing others. Let them teach you about the experience of loss, but also help clarify any damaging misconceptions they might have.
   ⇨ Dealing with parents' emotions: When you wonder why your child is acting in an unusual manner, ask yourself how you are feeling and coping?

• **Acceptance:** they can acknowledge the loss of their loved one and experience a balance of sadness coupled with the ability to reflect positively.

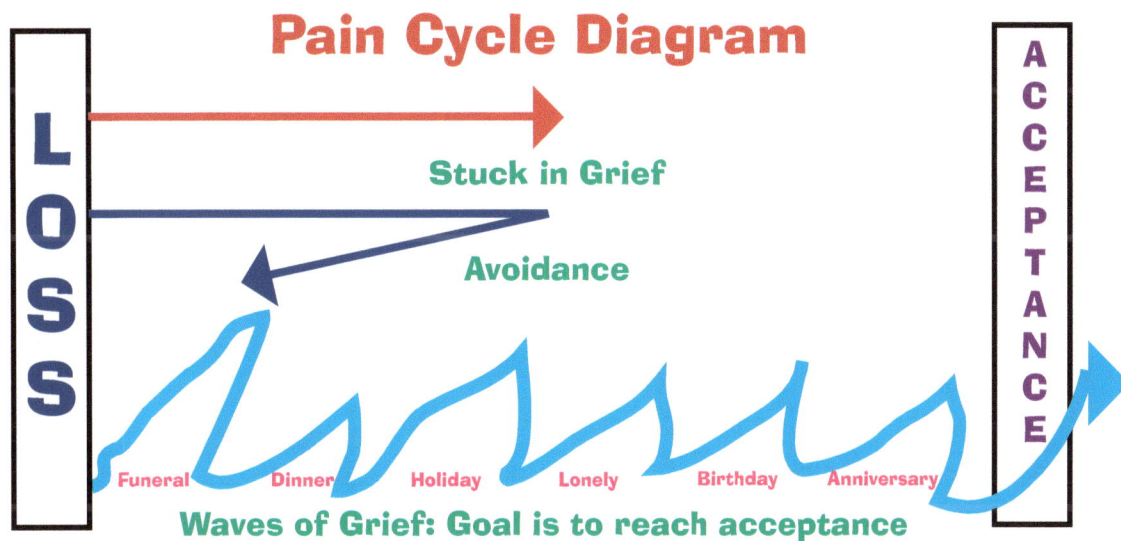

Pain Cycle Diagram

LOSS

Stuck in Grief

Avoidance

Funeral   Dinner   Holiday   Lonely   Birthday   Anniversary

ACCEPTANCE

Waves of Grief: Goal is to reach acceptance

Suggestions for Processing Emotional Reactions

• Create your own storybook of memories—positive, negative, funny, and sad.
• Let your children know how they are similar to the person they have lost.
• Create a memory box.
• Write letters (or poetry) to the deceased in a special journal.
• Symbolism—plant a tree, let balloons go, traditions at important events (birthdays, anniversary of the death), pick a symbol that reminds you of that person so every time you see it you are pleasantly reminded of them (i.e. music, butterfly, rainbow, etc.)
• Make families recipes that bring back warm memories.

Action Steps To Help Families Socially

Written by Amy McClenahan - Educator, Youth Mentor

Here are some communication tips that adults can try on the home and school fronts.

Feelings
- Grieving is a process that involves deep feelings.
- Recognize the grief both for yourself and your children, and the five stages of grieving that include feelings such as sad, mad, disbelief, anger and denial.
- Express your feelings; cry or be sad; and when asked by your child, put your feelings into words.
- In your child; look for any behavioral signs of sadness, anything out of the ordinary for your child, i.e. negative acting out or withdrawal. Ask feeling questions about the behavior such as "Are you feeling sad?" or "Do you miss Nana/Grandma?"

Talking
- Talk about the loved one who died, tell stories, share memories.
- For children ages ten and under, "indirect" talking is best, i.e. when driving in a car, doing a task together, shoulder to shoulder, during play, or on a walk.
- Consider your own beliefs about death and dying and how to discuss your values age appropriately. Many adults avoid the topic of death and dying, but it is a fact of life that should be discussed openly and as soon as the topic presents itself.
- Ask leading/open ended questions of each other, i.e., "What reminds you of Nana/Grandma?"

Listening
- Encourage children to share their own stories of the loved one.
- Sometimes children may not have words, but can draw a picture or act out a story.
- Create a photo book or collage of pictures and words together that remind you of your loved one.

Relief
- The feeling of relief is often normal. It is a sign that you cared enough about someone that you wanted their pain to end despite having to experience the pain of your loss.

What 2 Watch 4

Some red flags that indicate your child may not be handling the loss very well include:

- Incomplete Work: in-class/at-home assignments

- Attention-getting behavior, silliness, disrespectfulness, cursing, etc.

- Bed-wetting

- Attachment issues: crying when being dropped off at school, grandparents, child care, etc.

- Chronic Illness: stomach, head, muscle aches, etc.

- Withdrawal from friends, family, and hobbies/extra-curricular activities

- Anger Outbursts/Defiance

- Sleep Disturbances

- School Refusal

If you notice the warning signs above, please consider talking to your child about your concerns and then sharing them with a school counselor and/or psychologist to help your child resolve these issues more effectively.

Action Steps To Help Families Spiritually

Written by Mike McClenahan - Senior Pastor/Head of Staff at Solana Beach Presbyterian Church

Enter In

Grieving is hard and I haven't met a person who looks forward to grieving or assisting another person in their grief. When I walk into a hospital room, a mortuary, or a home, I'm never quite sure what the story will be. Will the other person grieve with anger, resignation, disappointment, gratitude, faith, or silence? What questions will they have? What do they need from me? What do I have to offer? For a parent or friend who is even less trained than a pastor, entering into another's pain and sadness can be very difficult and full of questions. But "Entering In" is the first step in helping another to grieve. Sometimes just being there, without saying a word, is the best thing any of us can do.

In the New Testament, the word compassion means to come alongside, to help with a heartfelt response, or to comfort. The apostle Paul uses that word when he writes to the early church "the Father of compassion and the God of all comfort, who comforts us in all our troubles, so that we can comfort those in any trouble with comfort we ourselves receive from God." (2 Corinthians 1:3-4). I like that image of walking alongside or entering into the journey with another. Whether it's a friend, a child, a spouse, or a neighbor, we enter into the story with others with faith that God enters in with us; they are not alone, and we are not alone.

Believe God One Step at a Time

I counseled a couple who lost their young daughter to a rare virus. She was a beautiful four-year-old with a beautiful smile and adventurous spirit. As I met with them, almost immediately they asked me, "Why did God take her?" and "Why is God punishing us?"

One of the hardest parts of my work as a pastor is around grief and God. Depending on the spiritual background, age, and experience of the person, the questions about God tend to focus around "why?" questions: "Why did God take my teenage son in that bike accident?" "Why did God take Nana with cancer at 59-years-old?" There are so many questions that either cannot be answered or cannot be answered yet. Without giving simplistic answers to complicated questions, I focus on simple faith statements we know to be true, and keep us on a spiritual journey through grief. The Bible, from beginning to end, affirms that God is always present and that God will never leave us, even in death (Exodus 3:12; John 16:33); God offers us life beyond death in heaven (John 11:25); that God comforts us in our pain (Psalm 23; Romans 8:38-39; Psalm 46); and scriptures also tell us God is love. (1 John 4:16; Lamentations 3:22).

Don Piper, in his book *Getting to Heaven: Departing Instructions For Your Life Now*, eloquently states the following from his personal experience of his *90 Minutes in Heaven*:

> "As I speak with thousands of people whose loved ones have passed away in the years since I returned from Heaven…I offer my sincere condolence 'for your temporary separation.' I often receive startled looks when I use the word temporary, but that's what it is. The separation is real, but it is only temporary," I point out. "You will be reunited with them. There is coming a great reunion someday. They have entered, not into death, but into eternal blessing."

We may not be able to believe all there is to believe at each step of the journey of grief, but we can focus on what we do believe. As we deal with our own grief, we can help children to affirm these simple faith statements that help them to know that trusting God is an important part of the journey.

Belong to Others in Community

I was nine-years-old when my three-year-old brother died. The week he was in the hospital people from church brought food to our home. The night he died in the hospital I was sitting in the living room with my family waiting for the news. Later our pastor sat in my room, in the dark, and prayed with my older brother and me. Over forty years later, my pastor's presence along with the support of my family and members of the community are the most prominent memory I have of that evening.

One way we can make faith real in times of grief is to engage in our spiritual community. Grieving causes us to isolate ourselves, afraid of expressing our emotions or uncertain that anyone else will understand our pain. We can feel guilty that our grief says we don't have enough faith in God. A spiritual community often provides a safe place to grieve. Questions can be asked, tears can be shed, and support can be offered in tangible ways through clergy, trained members, and casual friendships. A memorial service gives opportunity for celebration, grief, and seeking God together. Worship services can provide an opportunity to take steps of faith with others when it's hard or impossible to pray alone.

Once a mom told me that she sat in the back row of the sanctuary crying at every service. She would leave before the end of the service because she didn't want anyone to see her pain. Little by little she moved up a couple of rows towards the front of the sanctuary. She began meeting more people and became part of the church family.

We all have different capacities and needs for relationships in times of grief. Still adults and children need to know that even though their loved one died, they are still valued by the community and they have a place to be known and loved, to play, and to be included.

Build Memorials of Faith

Kristin was devastated to lose her brother in an Air Force training flight accident. As we met together, I shared with her a scripture verse from Isaiah 58:11, "You will be a well watered garden in a sun scorched land." That scripture had two promises for her journey of grief: it was going to be hard (like a desert) and God will be faithful (like a garden). That verse became a memorial of his death that gave her hope and faith.

A memorial is anything that reminds you of what God has done or what God will do. In the wilderness the people of God created name places and stone formations as memorials to God's faithfulness—a tangible reminder of God's faithfulness in difficult times. What memorial could you create with your family? A tree, garden, statue, picture, or collage can all serve as reminders of the person we lost and of God's faithfulness.

Everyone grieves differently, but God is always at work in us through our grief. These steps are not to be used the same in every circumstance, but can be thoughtfully and prayerfully used at appropriate times. The most important part is that families grieve together, with each other and with others, and learn to trust God through their grief.

Family prayers or bedtime prayers with children can be used to give thanks to God for the loved one and to grow in faith together. Parents can model faith for their children through honest, heartfelt prayers.

Dear God,

We ask for your help. You know we are sad because Nana died. We know that you are right here with us, that even though we are sad you will never leave us. We thank you for Nana, her smile, her cooking, her hugs. We know that Nana is with you in heaven and we look forward to seeing her again. Until then, we ask for your love, your peace, your comfort.

Amen

References for Adults:

- Freedman, Dr. Rita. *Overcoming Loss: A Guide to Healing.* New York: Peter Pauper Press, Inc, 1995.

- Kushner, Harold. *When Bad Things Happen to Good People.* New York: Avon Books - Imprint of HarperCollins, 1981.

- Pearson, Diane C. *God in the Midst of Grief.* Nashville: ACW Press, 2011.

- Piper, Don and Cecil Murphey. *90 Minutes in Heaven: A True Story of Death and Life and Death.* Grand Rapids, MI: Revel, 2004.

- Piper, Don and Cecil Murphey. *Getting to Heaven: Departing Instructions for Your Life Now.* New York: The Berkley Publishing Group, 2011.

- Russell, A.J. *God Calling.* Ohio: Barbour Publishing, Inc., 2011.

- Sittser, Gerald Lawson. *A Grace Disguised.* Michigan: Zondervan, 2004.

- Smith, John William. *Hugs for the Hurting.* Louisiana: Howard Publishing, 1997.

References for Children (Grade Level):

- Ryan, Victoria. *When Your Grandparent Dies: A Child's Guide to Good Grief.* Indiana: Abbey Press, 2002. **(all ages)**

- Schwiebert, Pat and Chuck DeKlyen. *Tear Soup: A Recipe for Healing After Loss.* Oregan: Grief Watch Group, 2005. **(all ages)**

- Shriver, Maria. *What's Heaven?* New York: St. Martin's Press, 2009. **(all ages)**

- Silverman. Janis. *Help Me Say Goodbye: Activities For Helping Kids Cope When a Special Person Dies.* Minnesota, Fairview Press, 1999. **(all ages)**

Web Links:

- Children's Grief Center
  www.childrensgrief.org

- Elisabeth Kubler-Ross Foundation
  www.ekrfoundation.org

- Hello Grief: an on-line community for teens
  www.hellogrief.org

- Gerard's House: A children's grief support group
  www.gerardshouse.org